Eli Manning

By Jeff Savage

AMAZING ATHLETES

Lerner Publications Company • Minneapolis

Lerner Publications Company
A division of Lerner Publishing Group, Inc.
241 First Avenue North
Minneapolis, MN 55401 U.S.A.

Website address: www.lernerbooks.com

Library of Congress Cataloging-in-Publication Data

Savage, Jeff, 1961–
    Eli Manning / by Jeff Savage.
        p.   cm. — (Amazing athlete)
    Includes bibliographical references and index.
    ISBN 978–0–7613–3984–7 (lib. bdg. : alk. paper)
    1. Manning, Eli, 1981– —Juvenile literature. 2. Football players—United States—Biography—
Juvenile literature. I. Title.
GV939.M289S267 2009
796.332092—dc22 [B]   2008018880

Manufactured in the United States of America
1 2 3 4 5 6 – BP – 14 13 12 11 10 09

TABLE OF CONTENTS

Eli throws a pass during the 2008 Super Bowl.

SUPER GAME

Eli Manning and the New York Giants had just two minutes, 39 seconds left in the 2008 **Super Bowl**. The Giants trailed the New England Patriots, 14–10. Patriots **quarterback** Tom Brady had just thrown a touchdown pass to Randy Moss. The Patriots were on the verge of becoming the first team in the National Football League (NFL) to have a perfect 19–0 season.

Eli had other ideas. In six plays, he moved the Giants up the field. Then on third down, Eli went back to pass. Patriots **defenders** swarmed around him. **Linemen** Jarvis Green and Richard Seymour grabbed his jersey. Somehow, Eli escaped.

Eli escapes a sack in one of the greatest moments in Super Bowl history.

Eli spun to his right and threw a pass down the middle of the field. **Wide receiver** David Tyree leaped and caught the football. Defender Rodney Harrison crashed into Tyree. As Tyree fell, he pinned the ball to his helmet to make a stunning catch. The Giants had reached the Patriots' 24-yard line. But the Giants still needed a touchdown to win the game. Time was running out.

David Tyree holds on to the ball as Rodney Harrison pulls him down.

With 45 seconds left, Eli calmly fired a pass to Steve Smith. Smith smartly got out of bounds at the 13-yard line to stop the clock. The Giants were out of timeouts. When Eli took the next snap, the Patriots **blitzed**. Eli lofted a perfect pass to the left corner of the **end zone**. Wide receiver Plaxico Burress was waiting for it. Burress caught the pass for the winning touchdown! The Giants had pulled off one of the greatest upsets in Super Bowl history. And Eli was named the game's Most Valuable Player (MVP)!

Plaxico Burress catches Eli's pass.

(Left to right) Peyton, Eli, and Cooper Manning wear jerseys in honor of their father. He had worn number 18 as quarterback at Ole Miss.

THE QUIET BROTHER

Elisha Nelson Manning was born January 3, 1981, in New Orleans, Louisiana. Eli was the youngest son of Archie and Olivia Manning. Archie had been the star quarterback at the University of Mississippi (nicknamed Ole Miss), where he met Olivia. He also played for fourteen years in the NFL, mostly for the New Orleans Saints. Eli's oldest brother, Cooper, played wide receiver in high school before a spinal problem cut short his career. Peyton, the next oldest, is the quarterback for the Indianapolis Colts. Naturally, Eli followed his father and brothers to the football field.

Peyton and Cooper were competitive growing up. Eli was quiet and shy. He liked to spend time with his mother. Archie often took the two older boys to sporting events. Olivia took Eli shopping. Peyton liked to pick on Eli. Cooper protected him.

Eli struggled to learn to read. He almost had to repeat the first grade. His parents switched him from Isidore Newman School, where his brothers went, to a smaller school. Eli's friends teased him. He worked hard to improve so he

Eli grew up in New Orleans, Louisiana.

could return to Newman. Eli rejoined Isidore Newman for eighth grade.

Eli was an outstanding athlete. But he was always humble. "Eli would come home from one of his baseball games and not say a word, and you'd ask him how it went," said his brother Cooper. "He'd say 'Good,' and not much more. We'd later find out that he'd hit a game-winning homer in the bottom of the ninth inning. If it was Peyton in the same situation, he'd barge through the front door and yell." Eli was more calm and laid-back than his brothers. He earned the nickname Easy.

Eli's nickname is Easy because he is easygoing. On the football field, he stays calm in a crisis. "When things are going bad, I've got to settle everyone down," Eli says. "I have to be the leader of the team."

Newman High School coach Frank Gendusa talks to Eli before a game.

Eli played quarterback for his school's **varsity** team for three years, just like Peyton before him. Eli threw for at least 2,000 yards and 20 touchdowns all three seasons. He finished his high school career with almost 200 more yards passing than Peyton. Dozens of colleges **recruited** Eli to play football for them. He chose his dad's former school, Ole Miss.

Ole Miss head coach David Cutcliffe encouraged Eli during the 2000 Music City Bowl game.

OLE MISS

Eli was a star at Ole Miss—but not at first. In 1999, he was **redshirted.** In 2000, he was a backup. In the fourth quarter of that season's final game—the Music City Bowl against West Virginia—he finally got a chance to play. He completed 12 of 20 passes for 167 yards and three touchdowns! Eli proved he was ready to lead the Ole Miss Rebels.

Eli guided Mississippi to a 6–1 record to start the 2001 season. Then, against Arkansas, he threw for 312 yards and six touchdowns. But the Rebels lost that game in seven **overtimes**, 58–56. In 2002, Eli led the Rebels to the Independence Bowl. They won 27–23 over Nebraska. But Eli saved his best for 2003. He led Ole Miss to a 10-win season, which included a 31–28 triumph over Oklahoma State in the Cotton Bowl.

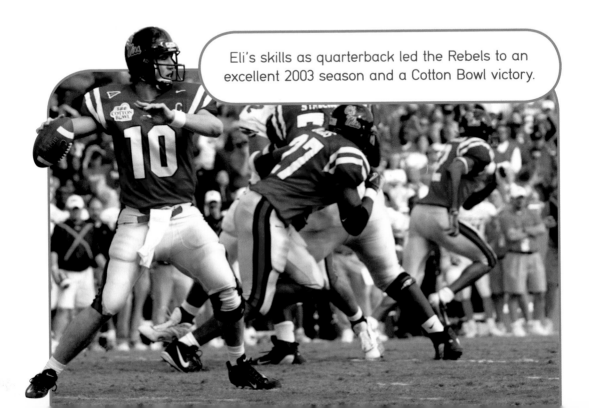

Eli's skills as quarterback led the Rebels to an excellent 2003 season and a Cotton Bowl victory.

Eli had set 47 passing records at Ole Miss. His play won him many honors, including the Maxwell Award as the nation's best all-around player.

Eli won the Maxwell Award in 2003.

Eli entered the NFL **Draft** in 2004. He seemed likely to be an NFL star. After all, Peyton had become a star for the Colts, and Archie was ready to offer guidance anytime.

The San Diego Chargers held the top pick in the draft. They had long been a losing team. They needed a quarterback. But Eli and his father made it clear that he did not want to play for the Chargers. San Diego chose Eli with the first pick anyway. Eli was heartbroken. He talked about quitting football.

Three picks later, the New York Giants chose quarterback Philip Rivers. Then came word of a trade. The Chargers traded Eli to the Giants for Rivers and three picks in the 2005 draft. The entire Manning family was thrilled. But Eli would have to show he was worth the trade.

Eli's family supported him at the 2004 NFL Draft. *From left*: Peyton and his wife, Ashley; Olivia; Eli's girlfriend (now wife), Abby McGrew; Eli; and Archie.

Eli played his first game as the Giants' starting quarterback against the Atlanta Falcons.

FINDING HIS WAY

Eli struggled as a **rookie**. The Giants plodded through the first half of the 2004 season with **veteran** Kurt Warner playing quarterback. Eli mostly watched from the sidelines. Midway through the year, coach Tom Coughlin decided to try Eli as his starting player.

A football game is like a three-hour "test." Before taking the test, Eli has to prepare. He studies films, goes to practice, and lifts weights. These efforts help him improve his play during the three hours he's on the field.

Eli threw his first NFL touchdown pass against the Atlanta Falcons. But he also threw two **interceptions**. The Giants lost that game and the next three. Against the Baltimore Ravens, Eli completed only four passes. New York's losing streak had reached eight games when the Giants faced the Dallas Cowboys in the season's final game. Eli led the offense on a last-minute touchdown drive to win, 28–24. Eli had shown a spark.

Eli worked hard in the off-season. He lifted weights. He studied the **playbook**. He watched **game film**. In 2005, the Giants officially named Eli the starting quarterback. He was ready. He led the team to victories over the Arizona Cardinals and the New Orleans Saints. Next, the Giants traveled to San Diego to play the Chargers.

San Diego fans had not forgotten that Eli had snubbed their team on draft day. They booed loudly every time he touched the ball. Eli stayed calm. He played his best game yet as a pro, passing for 352 yards and two touchdowns. But the Giants could not stop San Diego running back LaDainian Tomlinson. New York lost, 45–23.

San Diego Chargers fans were still upset that Eli had snubbed their team during the draft.

Eli played well during his first season. But the team had some disappointing losses.

The Giants returned home to face the St. Louis Rams. Eli torched the Rams' defense with four touchdown passes in a 44–24 victory.

Two games later, he led the offense on a last-minute drive against the Denver Broncos. Eli threw a touchdown strike to Amani Toomer with five seconds left. The Giants won, 24–23.

The Giants finished with an 11–5 record to make the playoffs.

Eli was near the top of the league in passing yards and touchdowns. Unfortunately, he also threw 17 interceptions and completed barely half his passes. Worse yet, he threw three more interceptions at home against the Carolina Panthers in the first round of the playoffs. The Giants lost, 23–0. They became the first playoff team in 25 years to go scoreless at home.

Carolina Panthers player Ken Lucas intercepts Eli's pass during the first round of the 2005 playoffs.

Eli *(left)* congratulates his brother. Peyton had just led the Colts to a victory over the Giants in 2006. Peyton also led his team to a Super Bowl Championship that season.

GIANT EXPECTATIONS

Giants fans were upset. They expected more from Eli. Newspaper reporters wrote negative stories about him. The criticism hurt Eli. But "Easy" Eli didn't get worked up. "You just have to learn to accept it," he said. "You have to . . . show everybody that . . . you are going to go out there and still practice hard and perform hard."

Eli's teammates admired his easygoing ways. He calmly led New York to a 6–2 record to start the 2006 season. Then injuries hit. Several Giants couldn't play. The losses piled up. New York finished the season with an 8–8 record. They barely made the playoffs and lost again in the first round.

Success in 2007 seemed unlikely. Star running back Tiki Barber retired before the season started. Defensive leader Michael Strahan talked of retiring. Key receiver Plaxico Burress was injured. The Giants lost their first two games, to the Dallas Cowboys and Green Bay Packers. Eli suffered a shoulder injury. Team owner John Mara questioned Eli's ability, saying, "Can we win with this guy?" Many fans wondered the same thing.

Coach Coughlin never doubted his quarterback. "Eli . . . is very focused on his job. He never bats an eye about what his responsibilities are."

In week three, the Giants rallied to win a game in Washington against the Redskins. Next, the defense shut down the Philadelphia

Giants head coach Tom Coughlin watches a play during the 2007 season.

Eagles with 12 **sacks**. To beat the New York Jets, Eli threw two second-half touchdowns. Then the Giants creamed the Falcons in a blowout on Monday Night Football. The

Giants kept rolling and earned another trip to the playoffs.

This time, the Giants took control. Eli completed 20 of 27 passes for two touchdowns at Tampa Bay. The Giants beat the Buccaneers, 24–14. At Dallas the following week, Eli calmly engineered a 21–17 upset over the Cowboys.

Eli throws a pass during the game against Tampa Bay.

The National Football Conference (NFC) Championship Game was in Green Bay, Wisconsin. The field was frozen. But Eli was red hot. Time after time, he moved the Giants into position to score. The game was tied, 20–20. Giants kicker Lawrence Tynes missed a late **field goal**. Then he missed another. Eli stayed Easy. In overtime, the Giants got into field goal position yet again. At last, Tynes made the kick. The Giants became the first NFC team to win three straight playoff games on the road. They were headed to the Super Bowl.

Eli calls a play during the chilly NFC Championship Game in Green Bay.

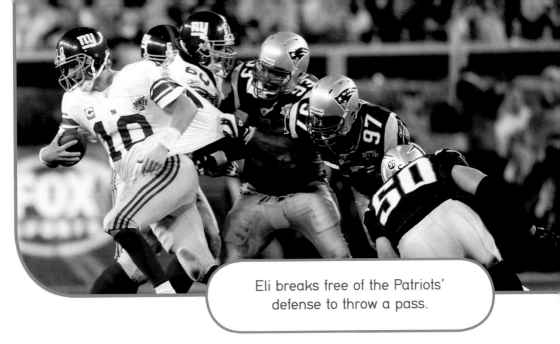

Eli breaks free of the Patriots' defense to throw a pass.

In Super Bowl XLII, the Patriots took a 7–3 lead on the first play of the second quarter. Neither team scored again until the fourth quarter. Eli threw a touchdown pass to David Tyree with 11:05 left. Patriots quarterback Tom Brady drove his team 80 yards to the end zone to retake the lead, 14–10. Once more, the pressure was on Eli. He swiftly moved the offense down the field and took back the game. New York won, 17–14. The Giants were Super Bowl champions!

Michael Strahan (left) and Eli hold their trophy at the Super Bowl parade in New York.

Eli had proved his doubters wrong. He said after the game that he often wondered if he deserved all the criticism he received. "So, to come out here and win," he added, "I'd have to say it is kind of sweet."

Eli married his college girlfriend, Abby McGrew, in 2008.

Selected Career Highlights

2007–2008 Super Bowl Most Valuable Player
Led New York Giants to Super Bowl title
Led Giants to NFC record three straight playoff road victories

2006 Matched career high with 24 touchdown passes

2005 Passed for career-high 3,762 yards and 24 touchdowns
Led Giants to 11–5 record and NFC East title

2004 Selected first in the NFL Draft
Made NFL debut against Philadelphia Eagles, completing three
  of nine passes for 66 yards

2003 Won Johnny Unitas Golden Arm Award as top college
  quarterback
Won Walter Camp Football Foundation Player of the Year Award
Named First Team All-America
Named Southeastern Conference Player of the Year

2002 Named to the Southeastern Conference Academic Honor Roll

2001 Named to the Southeastern Conference Academic Honor Roll
Won Conerly Trophy as Best College Football Player
  in Mississippi

2000 Named to the Southeastern Conference Academic Honor Roll

1998 Named to High School
  All-America team
Named USA TODAY State
  Player of the Year in
  Louisiana

Glossary

blitzed: sent extra defensive players to rush the quarterback

defenders: players whose job it is to try to stop the other team from scoring points

draft: a yearly event in which professional teams take turns choosing new players from a selected group

end zone: the area beyond the goal line at either end of the field. To score, a team tries to get the ball into the other team's end zone.

field goal: a successful kick over the U-shaped upright poles. A field goal is worth three points.

game film: videotape of a game that players and coaches study

interceptions: passes caught by a player on the defense. An interception results in the opposing team getting control of the ball.

linemen: players who are positioned at the line where the play begins

overtimes: extra periods of play to break a tie. In college football, each team is given one possession to score. If both teams score an equal number of points, another overtime is played. In pro football, the first team to score wins.

playbook: descriptions of a team's offensive and defensive plays

quarterback: the person who throws or hands off the ball

recruited: offered a chance to play on a team by a scout searching for players

redshirted: made to sit out for the first year on a college team to learn. A player starts his college career in the second year and is still allowed to play for four years.

rookie: a first-year player

sacks: plays in which the quarterback is tackled behind the yard line where the play began, before the football is thrown or handed off

Super Bowl: the final game of each season between the champions of the American Football Conference and the National Football Conference. The winner of the Super Bowl is that season's NFL champion.

varsity: the top level in ability of a school team, above the junior varsity and freshman teams

veteran: a player with two or more years of experience

wide receiver: a player who catches passes, mainly for a big gain

Further Reading & Websites

Sandler, Michael. *Eli Manning and the New York Giants: Super Bowl XLII*. New York: Bearport Publishing, 2009.

Savage, Jeff. *Peyton Manning*. Rev. Ed. Minneapolis: Lerner Publications Company, 2008.

Savage, Jeff. *Tom Brady*. Rev. Ed. Minneapolis: Lerner Publications Company, 2009.

Tieck, Sarah. *Eli Manning*. Edina, MN: ABDO Publishing Company, 2009.

Eli's Website
http://www.elimanning.com
Eli's official website, featuring news, records, photos, trivia, and other information about Eli and his family.

Official NFL Site
http://www.nfl.com
The official National Football League website provides fans with game action, statistics, schedules, and biographies of players.

Sports Illustrated Kids
http://www.sikids.com
The *Sports Illustrated Kids* website covers all sports, including football.

Index

Photo Acknowledgments

The images in this book are used with the permission of: AP Photo/Paul Sancya, pp. 4, 24; © Jay Drowns/Sporting News/ZUMA Press, p. 5; AP Photo/ Elaine Thompson, p. 6; AP Photo/Ross B. Franklin, p. 7; © Michael C. Herbert/ US Presswire, p. 8; © Prisma/SuperStock, p. 10; AP Photo/David Rae Morris, p. 12; AP Photo/Wade Payne, p. 13; © Ronald Martinez/Getty Images, p. 14; AP Photo/Scott Audette, p. 15; © Chris Trotman/Getty Images, p. 16; © John Dunn/USP/ZUMA Press, p. 17; © Stephen Dunn/Getty Images, p. 19; AP Photo/Kathy Willens, p. 20; © Tom Berg/NFL/Getty Images, p. 21; © Travis Lindquist/Getty Images, p. 22; AP Photo/Steve Nesius, p. 25; © Jamie Squire/ Getty Images, p. 26; © Andy Lyons/Getty Images, p. 27; AP Photo/Frank Franklin II, p. 28; AP Photo/Jeff Roberson, p. 29.

Front Cover: © Evan Pinkus/Getty Images.